D0886619

Immortal Jester

'*Winston was a man of wit and chuckling humour* . . .'

– The Right Hon Sir Robert Menzies,
30th January, 1965

Immortal Jester

A Treasury of
The Great Good Humour of

SIR WINSTON CHURCHILL, KG, OM, CH

1874-1965

Compiled by Leslie Frewin

LESLIE FREWIN of LONDON

For Sarah of The Empty Spaces

First published 1973 by
Leslie Frewin Publishers Limited,
Five Goodwin's Court,
Saint Martin's Lane,
London WC2N 4LL, England.

This book is set in Bembo 12/14 pt.
Printed and bound by
R. J. Acford Limited,
Industrial Estate,
Chichester, Sussex, England.

ISBN 0 85632 031 5

'He is history's child, and
what he said and
what he did will never die'

–The late General de Gaulle
on the death of Sir Winston Churchill

Churchill – Minister of the Crown

12th December 1905 to 5th April 1908:
Under-Secretary of State for Colonies – *Liberal* (Sir Henry Campbell-Bannerman)

12th April 1908 to 14th February 1910:
President, Board of Trade – *Liberal* (H H Asquith)

14th February 1910 to 23rd October 1911:
Home Secretary – *Liberal* (H H Asquith)

23rd October 1911 to 25th May 1915:
First Lord of the Admiralty – *Liberal* (H H Asquith)

25th May 1915 to 12th November 1915:
Chancellor of the Duchy of Lancaster – *Coalition* (H H Asquith)

15th July 1917 to 10th January 1919:
Minister of Munitions – *Coalition* (D Lloyd George)

10th January 1919 to 13th February 1921:
Secretary of State for War and Air – *Coalition* (D Lloyd George)

13th February 1921 to 1st April 1921:
Secretary of State for Colonies and Air – *Coalition* (D Lloyd George)

1st April 1921 to 23rd October 1922:
Secretary of State for Colonies – *Coalition* (D Lloyd George)

6th November 1924 to 4th June 1929:
Chancellor of the Exchequer – *Conservative* (Stanley Baldwin)

3rd September 1939 to 10th May 1940:
First Lord of the Admiralty – *National* (Neville Chamberlain)

10th May 1940 to 23rd May 1945:
Prime Minister and Minister of Defence – *Coalition*

23rd May 1945 to 26th July 1945:
Prime Minister and Minister of Defence – *Conservative*

26th October 1951 to 28th October 1951:
Prime Minister – *Conservative*

28th October 1951 to 1st March 1952:
Prime Minister and Minister of Defence – *Conservative*

1st March 1952 to 5th April 1955:
Prime Minister – *Conservative*

Contents

	Page
Introduction	11
On Himself	14
On Women	22
On People	26
On The British Empire and its People	36
On the Economy	42
On Politics and Politicians	48
On Socialism and Socialists	54
On Other Nations	60

5

CONTENTS

	Page
On Democracy	68
On Dictators	72
On Arms and the Armed Forces	76
On Invasion	84
On War	90
On Diplomacy	96
On Truth	100
On Words	104
On Making Speeches	114
On Pastimes	120
On Religion	124
On Life	128
On Danger, Defeat and Death	134

List of Illustrations

Between pages 28 and 29

Churchill with Mrs Churchill (C), Charlie Chaplin (*far R*) and members of a Chartwell house party; 19th September 1931.

Winston is carried into his London flat after a spell in a nursing home following paratyphoid; 10th October 1932.

Mr and Mrs Churchill and Lady Oxford leaving the stage door of the Apollo Theatre on 12th January 1943, after seeing Terence Rattigan's play *Flare Path*.

A bit of history. Winston Churchill (R) with Lloyd George at a farewell party to the Chinese Ambassador. London, 1941.

The famous victory sign for British seamen as he disembarks for his 1943 American visit.

Stalin grins at a Churchill witticism; Yalta, February 1945.

With Joseph Stalin and Franklin D Roosevelt at one of the Teheran conferences.

LIST OF ILLUSTRATIONS

Between pages 28 and 29

Winston, with Ernest Bevin (L) and Sir John Anderson, makes a triumphant VE-Day appearance on the balcony of the Ministry of Health, London; 8th May 1945.

A war-time picture in Paris with General 'Ike' Eisenhower at Supreme Allied Headquarters, shortly after the liberation of the French capital.

A visit to the French Embassy in London. Sir Winston with the French Ambassador and Junior Commander Mary Churchill. May 1945.

The historic picture of Winston Churchill striding the Champs Elysées in Paris with General Charles de Gaulle after the liberation of the city.

Between pages 44 and 45

A rest on Hitler's chair outside the ruins of the Fuhrer's air raid shelter in Berlin at the end of World War II. The Russian officers in the foreground share the enjoyment of the scene.

Acknowledging the cheers of the Ayr, Scotland, crowds after receiving the Freedom of the Burgh; 15th May 1947.

With Lord Beaverbrook – 'The Beaver' – aboard HMS *Prince of Wales*.

Artist at work. Sir Winston painting above the little fishing village of Camara da Lobus, Funchal. The lady in the picture is Mrs C B Nairn, wife of the then British Consul in Madeira. 1950.

As host to Margaret, daughter of President Truman (*second from R*). Also in this group at Chartwell, 4th June 1951, are Mr and Mrs Walter Gifford (L), Mary (Churchill) and husband Christopher Soames.

Arrival in Glasgow to address vast crowds at a Conservative Election meeting – with that old familiar greeting . . .

Churchill speaks, the crowd roars: the Royal Wanstead School Fête, 21st July 1951.

A beaming Winston at the 1952 christening of his eighth grandchild, Jeremy Soames, son of daughter Mary. (Field Marshal Montgomery was godfather.)

Between pages 60 and 61

Field Marshal Montgomery (*second R*) and General Eisenhower (*R*) with Winston at the El Alamein Reunion, London; 19th October 1951. (Presenting the cigar is stage producer Ralph Reader.)

As Chancellor of Bristol University. 14th December 1951.

President Truman and Churchill with a painting of US Frigate *Constitution* firing on HMS *Java* in the 1812 War. Aboard the Presidential Yacht; 6th January 1952.

LIST OF ILLUSTRATIONS

Between pages 60 and 61

Embarking for the United States, with his son-in-law Christopher Soames. 30th December 1952.

Turkish Premier Adnan Menderes, in London, 14th October 1952, enjoys a Churchill story.

Prince Philip, Duke of Edinburgh, with General Matthew B Ridgeway, then Supreme Commander, Allied Powers in Europe, and Sir Winston at The Pilgrims' Dinner. Savoy Hotel, London, 1952.

Two farewells . . .
(L) to Ethiopian Emperor Haile Selassie, after lunch at 10 Downing Street, 22nd October 1954.
(B) to President Eisenhower after a visit to The White House, 29th June 1954.

In lively discussion with King Gustav of Sweden, shortly after Sir Winston's Nobel Prize Award for Literature; 11th November 1953.

Between pages 76 and 77

Queen Elizabeth and Prince Philip leave 'Number Ten' after a dinner party; 4th April 1955.

The statesman poses with the Mayor of Hastings after being presented with a portrait of himself from the Cinque Ports and associated towns.

The statesman is visited at his Chartwell home by seven proud officers and forty equally proud other ranks of the 5th (Cinque Ports) Battalion of The Royal Sussex Regiment, TA. Lady Churchill is seen in the background with three of her grandchildren. Kent, April 1956.

Sir Anthony Eden, then the British Prime Minister, receives his mentor, Winston Churchill, at No. 10 Downing Street. London, November 1956.

Sir Winston goes in to receive The Charlemagne Prize for his services to Western Europe. Aachen, May 1956.

Sir Winston arrives in Nice . . . and, unexpectedly, pouring rain! 7th March 1959.

April 1959, the French Riviera. Sir Winston enjoys a visit to his neighbour, Somerset Maugham.

October 1959, Woodford. Sir Winston stops in his election campaign to greet a famous constituent, tennis star Christine Truman.

Sir Winston and Lady Churchill, Harrow School Speech Day; 16th November 1961.

Sir Winston greets the American Ambassador to London, Mr David Bruce, after receiving his American passport on being made an honorary citizen of the United States. London, April 1963.

9

LIST OF ILLUSTRATIONS

Between pages 116 and 117

Muffled against the cold and rain, Sir Winston leaves his Hyde Park Gate, London, home for the House of Commons, 14th May 1963, after nearly a year's absence from Parliament.

'My Darling Clementine' . . . Sir Winston and Lady Churchill on the occasion of Lady Churchill's 78th Birthday, 1st April 1963.

Sir Winston appears at the window of his London home on his 89th birthday; 30th November 1963.

Introduction

There has surely been no other statesman so masterful at manipulating the English language as Sir Winston Churchill. Politician and prophet, he was one of the greatest writers and orators of this century, who delivered, during his ninety years, countless words on just about every subject of concern to mankind.

His insight and wisdom show him to be a humanist with, above all, a sense of humour and wit unequalled in any of his political adversaries. With a deft flick of the pen or tongue he was able to turn a phrase or make a comment that could reduce the most serious situation to gales of laughter or bring shades of embarrassment to a less voluble opponent. In just one such situation, in the

II

House of Commons, Churchill, seemingly benevolent, described Herbert Morrison as a 'master of craftsmen'. Morrison, quiet taken aback by the unexpected compliment, said: 'The right honorable Gentleman has promoted me.' To which Churchill, in a flash, replied: 'Yes, but craft is common both to skill and deceit.'

Sometimes barbed and cutting, sometimes devastatingly rude, sometimes whimsical, at all times extremely funny, Churchill's knack with metaphor, simile, innuendo and other literary devices was nothing short of brilliant. This book is an attempt to record some of that brilliance. In it will be found oft-quoted and more obscure extracts from speeches and letters; *bons mots*, asides and off-the-cuff remarks during political debates and on other occasions which, I believe, all reveal the vigorous, towering mind of the 'Immortal Jester'.

London, 1973.   LF

On Himself

On Himself

The young Churchill was a 'troublesome boy':
'Churchill, I have very grave reason to be displeased with you,' said the headmaster of Harrow School once in reprimand.
'And I, sir, have very grave reason to be displeased with you', the impudent pupil replied.

*　　*　　*

Winston once summoned a parlourmaid to his room where he was taking a lesson with his governess, Miss Hutchinson. The maid was most surprised when the boy said:
'Please take Miss Hutchinson away. She is very cross.'

*　　*　　*

At school, Churchill found mathematics a most difficult subject:
'The figures were tied in all sorts of tangles and did things to one another which it was extremely difficult to forecast.'

*　　*　　*

His love for the English language brought this comment:

'I am biased in favour of boys learning English. I would let the clever ones learn Latin as an honour, and Greek as a treat. But the only thing I would whip them for is for not knowing English. I would whip them hard for that.'

*   *   *

He was a man who found it difficult to arrive anywhere on time:

'I do think unpunctuality is a vile habit, and all my life I have been trying to break myself of it. The only straightforward course is to cut out one or two of the appointments and so catch up. But few men have the strength of mind to do this. It is better that one notability should be turned away expostulating from the doorstep, than that nine just deputations should each fume for ten minutes in a stuffy anteroom.'

*   *   *

Asked why he always seemed to miss trains and airplanes, he said:

'I am a sporting man. I always give them a fair chance of getting away!'

*   *   *

About his boundless energy, he said:

'I am certainly not one of those who need to be prodded. In fact, if anything, I am a prod.'

                                       – Commons, London. 11th November 1942

*   *   *

'*Because I show robust energy, it does not follow that I have a sensitive or injured disposition.*'

– Commons, London. 23rd April 1953

*   *   *

A much criticised man, he said of this:
'*I have derived continued benefit from criticism at all periods of my life, and, I do not remember any time when I was ever short of it.*'

– 27th November 1914

*   *   *

'*Criticism may not be agreeable, but it is necessary.   It fulfils the same function as pain in the human body, it calls attention to the development of an unhealthy state of things.*'

*   *   *

'*Personally I am always ready to learn, although I do not always like being taught.*'

*   *   *

'*So long as I am acting from duty and conviction, I am indifferent to taunts and jeers.   I think they will probably do me more good than harm.*'

– Commons, London. 6th December 1945

*   *   *

'*It is no part of my case that I am always right.*'
– Commons, London. 21st May 1952

*　　*　　*

'*My views are a harmonious process which keeps them in relation to the current movement of events.*'

*　　*　　*

'*I have today to deal with a motion of censure and therefore I hope I shall be pardoned if I do not confine myself entirely to the uncontroversial methods which I usually practise.*
– Commons, London. 4th December 1952

*　　*　　*

'*My conscience is a good girl. I can always come to terms with her.*'

*　　*　　*

'*I am very well accustomed to weigh expert evidence, and most of the important decisions which have been taken in the last three or four years at the Admiralty have been taken by me on a divergence of expert evidence.*'
– Commons, London. 15th November 1915

*　　*　　*

'*I always avoid prophesying beforehand, because it is much better policy to prophesy after the event has already taken place.*

* * *

'*I have no intention of passing my remaining years in explaining or withdrawing anything I have said in the past, still less in apologising for it.*'

* * *

He once called himself an 'English Speaking Union' because his mother was American and his ancestors officers in Washington's army.

* * *

In July 1939, Churchill met Fabian von Schlabrendorff. The German opened the conversation with:
'*I am not a Nazi, but a good patriot.*'
'*So am I*', replied a grinning Churchill.

* * *

He had much to say on being Prime Minister:
'*The dignity of a Prime Minister, like a lady's virtue, is not susceptible of partial diminution.*'

– *Commons, London. July 1905*

* * *

'When I was called upon to be Prime Minister, now nearly two years ago, there were not many applicants for the job. Since then perhaps the market has improved.'

– Commons, London. *January 1942*

* * *

'We mean to hold our own. I have not become the King's First Minister in order to preside over the liquidation of the British Empire. For that task, if ever it were prescribed, someone else would have to be consulted.'

– Mansion House, London. *10th November 1942*

* * *

'This is the first occasion when I have addressed this assembly here as Prime Minister. The explanation is convincing. When I should have come here as Prime Minister, the Guildhall was blown up and before it was repaired, I was blown out.'

– Guildhall, London. *1951*

* * *

In retrospect on his role as Prime Minister during the Second World War:

'I have never accepted what many people have kindly said, namely that I inspired the nation. Their will was resolute and remorseless, and as it proved, unconquerable ... It was the nation and the race dwelling all round the globe that had the lion's heart. I had the luck to be called upon to give the roar!'

* * *

19

Asked if he had made plans to retire, he said:

'*Not until I am a great deal worse and the Empire is a great deal better.*'

On Women

On Women

'In September, 1908, I married and lived happily ever after.'

*　　*　　*

When asked by an American feminist for his feelings on equality between the sexes and what Woman's future role should be in the future, he reflectively replied:

'The same, I trust, as it has been since the days of Adam and Eve.'

*　　*　　*

'Winston, you're drunk', said Bessie Braddock, Socialist member for Liverpool.

'Bessie, you're ugly and tomorrow morning I'll be sober but you'll still be ugly', retorted Churchill.

– Commons, London

*　　*　　*

'*It is hard, if not impossible, to snub a beautiful woman – they remain beautiful and the rebuke recoils.*'

* * *

'*If you were my husband, I'd poison your coffee*': Lady Astor to Churchill.
'*If you were my wife, I'd drink it*': Churchill to Lady Astor.

* * *

'*Mr Churchill, I care for neither your politics nor your moustache*', remarked a young female dinner companion to the newly-bewhiskered Churchill.
'*Don't distress yourself*', he replied, '*you are not likely to come in contact with either.*'

* * *

One of Churchill's most famous remarks about women came when he addressed a female member of Parliament as 'Sir'. When asked if he should not have begun his reply with 'Madam', he answered:
'*Man embraces woman*'.

On People

On People

'*We cannot have a band of drones in our midst, whether they come from the ancient aristocracy or the modern plutocracy or the ordinary type of pub crawler.*'

– London. *21st March 1943*

*   *   *

Sir Stafford Cripps was one of Churchill's longtime political adversaries. A dour, austere man who preferred not to eat meat, he was often the target for Churchill's wit:

'*Everyone knows the distinguished talents which the right honourable gentleman brings unstintingly to the services of his fellow countrymen. No one has made more sustained exertions to the common pot and few take less out of it than he does*'.

*   *   *

'I have got my vegetarian, too, my honoured friend, Lord Cherwell. These ethereal beings certainly do produce a very high level and a great volume of intellectual output, with a minimum of working costs and fuel.'

– During the post-war meat shortage

*   *   *

'I am glad I am not a herbivore. I eat what I like, I drink what I like, I do what I like . . . and he's *(Sir Stafford Cripps) the one to have a red nose.'*

*   *   *

'It is perhaps as well that I was not accompanied by my colleague, the Minister of Aircraft Production (Sir Stafford Cripps), for there is a man who habitually takes his meal of a handful of peas, and, when he gets a handful of beans, counts them his Christmas feast.'

*   *   *

Finding himself near Sir Stafford Cripps at dinner, he turned and said to a neighbour:
  'Who will relieve me of this Wuthering Height?'

*   *   *

Talking about the Greek General Plastiras, Churchill exclaimed:
'*Plasterarse, eh? Well, I hope at least he hasn't got feet of clay.*'
– *During the Greek Civil War. 1944*

*   *   *

'*Extremists made the infinite complexities of scientific civilisation and the multitudinous phenomena of great cities conform to a few barbarous formulas which any moderately intelligent parrot could repeat in a fortnight.*'

*   *   *

'*King Farouk was wallowing like a sow in a trough of luxury.*'

*   *   *

'*Dr Hugh Dalton – the practitioner who never cured anyone.*'

*   *   *

Bottom photograph opposite:
The photographer tells a story with this picture: 'I had asked the great man's detective whether I could take a picture and he bluntly told me that Mr Churchill didn't want any photographs taken. I said, "But Mr Churchill knows me. If you ask him he won't refuse." The detective replied, "And I know you, too! You can't take any pictures!" As luck would have it, the door opened and Mr Churchill, his wife and Lady Oxford came out. The detective said, "You don't want any pictures taken, do you, sir?" Much to his surprise (and mine!) the Prime Minister said, "Yes, yes, yes. Let him take one." I hurriedly got off three shots and these appeared in the next morning's papers. That night Mr Churchill flew secretly to Casablanca. He had quick-wittedly used me to "confuse and mislead the enemy", as the Army phrase has it.'

*   *   *

Churchill with Mrs Churchill (*C*), Charlie Chaplin (*far R*) and members of a Chartwell house party; 19th September 1931.

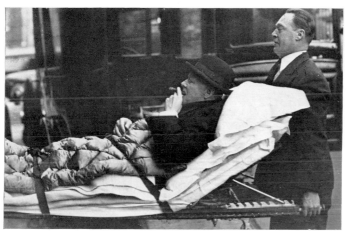

Winston is carried into his London flat after a spell in a nursing home following paratyphoid; 10th October 1932.

Mr and Mrs Churchill and Lady Oxford leaving the stage door of the Apollo Theatre on 12th January 1943, after seeing Terence Rattigan's play *Flare Path*.

A bit of history. Winston Churchi[ll]
(R) with Lloyd George at a farewe[ll]
party to the Chinese Ambassador.
London, 1941.

The famous victory sign for British
seamen as he disembarks for his
American visit.

...n grins at a Churchill
...icism; Yalta,
...uary 1945.

...h Joseph Stalin and
...klin D Roosevelt at
...of the Teheran
...erences.

...ston, with Ernest
...n (L) and Sir John
...erson, makes a
...mphant VE-Day
...arance on the balcony
...e Ministry of Health,
...don; 8th May 1945.

A war-time picture in Paris with General 'Ike' Eisenhower at Supr Allied Headquarters, shortly after th liberation of the French capital.

A visit to the French Embassy in London. Sir Winston with the Fr Ambassador and Junior Commander Mary Churchill. May 1945.

The historic picture of Winston Churchill striding the Champs Elysé Paris with General Charles de Gaull after the liberation of the city.

Charles Masterman MP was telling Churchill how much he admired Keir Hardie. He said:

'*He is not a great politician but he will be in heaven before either you or me, Winston!*'

To which Churchill replied:

'*If heaven is going to be full of people like Hardie, well, the Almighty can have them to himself.*'

*   *   *

About Clement Attlee, he remarked:

'*He is a sheep in sheep's clothing.*'

And:

'*Mr Attlee is a modest man. But then he has much to be modest about.*'

*   *   *

'*In looking at the views of these two honourable members (the brothers Sir Edgar Vincent and Sir C E H Vincent) I have always marvelled at the economy of nature which had contrived to grow from a single stock the nettle and the dock.*'

– Commons, London. 24th July 1905

*   *   *

'*Everyone has his day and some days last longer than others.*'

– Commons, London. January 1952

*   *   *

During a speech at the Oxford Union, Churchill described the economist Sir Arthur Salter as:

'A most engaging gentleman and a great authority on economic subjects. But like all of us he makes his mistakes from time to time. There was an instance when he eulogised highly the late Mr Ivar Kreuger as one of the financial greats of the world, who had blazed a trail along which men should follow. While the book was still in print, Mr Kreuger found it necessary to commit suicide because of his gigantic frauds. This was one instance when Sir Arthur's judgement did not actually hit the bull's-eye or even the circle.'

*   *   *

'The difference between Balfour and Asquith is that Arthur is wicked and moral, Asquith is good and immoral.'

*   *   *

Churchill's suggested slogan for Al Smith who was running for the Presidency of the United States was:

'All for Al, and Al for All.'

*   *   *

'It is alarming and nauseating to see Mr Gandhi, a seditious Middle Temple lawyer, now posing as a fakir of a type well known in the East, striding half naked up the steps of the Vice-Regal Palace, while he is still organising and conducting a defiant campaign of civil disobedience, to parley on equal terms with the representative of the King-Emperor.'

*   *   *

'*Lenin was sent into Russia by the Germans in the same way that you might send a phial containing a culture of typhoid or cholera to be poured into the water supply of a great city.*'

> – *Commons, London. November 1919*

* * *

'*I love a womanly woman and I admire a manly man but I cannot bear a boily boy.*'

* * *

Some of Churchill's more scathing comments were aimed at Ramsay MacDonald:

'*I remember when I was a child being taken to the celebrated Barnum's Circus, which contained an exhibition of freaks and monstrosities, but the exhibit on the programme which I desired to see was the one described as "The Boneless Wonder".*

My parents judged that spectacle would be too revolting and demoralising for my youthful eyes, and I have waited fifty years to see "The Boneless Wonder" sitting on the Treasury Bench.'

> – *Commons, London. 1931*

* * *

And when MacDonald became Prime Minister:

'*We know that he has, more than any other man, the gift of compressing the largest amount of words into the smallest amount of thought.*'

* * *

Describing his relationship with Lord Beaverbrook, he said:
  '*Max is a foul-weather friend.*'

* * *

  '*If you recognise anyone it does not mean that you like him. We all, for instance, recognise the right honourable gentleman the Member for Ebbw Vale (Mr Aneurin Bevan).*'

* * *

  Churchill: '*I am all for the social order.*'
  Lloyd George: '*No! I am against it.*'
  Churchill: '*You are not against the social order but only those parts of it which get in your way.*'

* * *

A new MP, Sir Alfred Bossom, had entered the House of Commons:
  '*Bossom?*', said Churchill, '*Bossom? What an extraordinary name . . . neither one thing nor the other!*'

* * *

  '*Mr Chamberlain loves the working man, he loves to see him work.*'

* * *

'*Who is this man Damaskinos? Is he a scheming, medieval prelate? Then he's our man.*'

*   *   *

'*I should advise the right honourable Gentleman (Mr Arnold Foster, Secretary of State for War) not to worry too much about details, because, after all, there would be an election some day, and when it came the waters of the boundless ocean would come in and all the castles on the sands would be washed away.*'

— *Commons, London. 23rd February 1905*

*   *   *

Describing General de Gaulle during the war, he said:
    '*The heaviest cross I have to bear is the Cross of Lorraine.*'

*   *   *

'*I hold no brief for Admiral Darlan. Like myself he is the object of the animosities of Herr Hitler and of Monsieur Laval. Otherwise I have nothing in common with him.*'

— *Commons, London. 10th December 1942*

*   *   *

Churchill once said that David Lloyd George could 'talk a bird out of a tree'.

*   *   *

He once wrote of Sir William Joynson Hicks:

'*The worst that can be said about him is that he runs the risk of being most humorous when he wishes to be most serious.*'

* * *

'*It might be said that Lord Rosebery outlived his future by ten years and his past by more than twenty.*'

* * *

Writing about Mr Stanley Baldwin, a former British Prime Minister:

'*In those days, Mr Baldwin was wiser than he is now, he used frequently to take my advice.*'

And:

'*Everybody who knew him loved him. This last must always be considered a dubious qualification.*'

On the British
Empire and its
People

On the British Empire and its People

'The British Constitution is mainly British common sense.'
— Kinnaird Hall, Dundee. 14th May 1908

* * *

'Britain, like any other country, is always changing but, like nature, never draws a line without smudging it.'
— Ayr. 16th May 1947

* * *

'The British people have always been superior to the British climate. They have shown themselves capable of rising above it.'
— Woodford Green. 10th July 1948

* * *

Describing British naval strategy in 1914, he said:
'The nose of the bulldog has been slanted backwards so that he can breathe without letting go.'

*   *   *

'Already, Mr Gandhi moves about surrounded by a circle of wealthy men who see at their fingertips the acquisition of an Empire on cheaper terms than were ever yet offered in the world. Sir, the Roman senator, Didius Julianus, was dining in a restaurant when they told him that the Praetorian Guard put the Empire up to auction and were selling it in the ditch in their camp; he ran out, and, according to Gibbon, bought it for £200 sterling per soldier. That was fairly cheap; but the terms upon which the Empire is being offered to this group surrounding Mr Gandhi are cheaper still.'

– Commons, London. 12th March 1931

*   *   *

'Here in this country we know that no dark designs are harboured by our Government against the peace or well-being of any country. There may be mistakes, there may be muddles, but no dark designs are harboured by any British Prime Minister or Foreign Secretary. He could not live under the conditions of British Cabinet Government if it were otherwise. But foreign countries do not always attribute to us this innocence.'

– Commons, London. 13th April 1933

*   *   *

'*When the British people make up their minds to go to war they expect to receive terrible injuries. That is why we tried to remain at peace as long as possible.*'

– *Commons, London. 5th September 1940*

*   *   *

'*Personally I think that private property has a right to be defended. Our civilisation is built up on private property, and can only be defended by private property.*'

*   *   *

'*When I warned the French that Britain would fight on alone whatever they did, their Generals told their Prime Minister and his divided Cabinet:* "In three weeks, England will have her neck wrung like a chicken".'

'*Some chicken, some neck.*'

– *Commons, London. December 1951*

*   *   *

'*What we are faced with is not a violent jerk but a prolonged pull.*'

– *Commons, London. 1953*

*   *   *

'*We used to be a source of fuel; we are increasingly becoming a sink.*'

– *Commons, London. 24th April 1928*

*   *   *

'Frightfulness *is not a remedy known to the British pharmacopœia.*'
                    – *Commons, London. 8th July 1920*

*   *   *

Mr Gower (Conservative):
  '*Can the Prime Minister state what course will be followed if a future British monarch should bear the name Llewellyn?*'
The Prime Minister:
  '*I hope I may ask for long notice of this question.*'

*   *   *

And on another royal topic, that of the arrangements for the Coronation of Queen Elizabeth II, he had this to say about the suggestion from Mr Glanville (Labour) that contingents representing all aspects of industry and industrial life be included in the procession:
  '*The arrangements for the procession are in the hands of the Coronation Committee and I expect that they will recommend that only military formations should be included.*'
  '*Why?*' asked Mr Glanville. To which Churchill replied:
  '*You must think of the spectators.*'
                    – *Commons, London. 1952*

39

On the Economy

On the Economy

'*I am very glad the House allowed me, after an interval of fifteen years, to lift again the tattered flag of retrenchment and economy.*'
                                              – Commons, London. 13th May 1901

*   *   *

'*Expenditure always is popular; the only unpopular part about it is the raising of the money to pay the expenditure.*'
                                              – Commons, London. 13th May 1901

*   *   *

'*If in the realm of the very poor any economy is possible, which I do not assert, there would be more likely to be economy possible over a crust of bread than over a spoonful of tea.*'
                                              – Commons, London. 12th May 1902

*   *   *

'*Those who dealt in guineas were not usually of the impoverished classes.*'

— *Commons, London. 26th June 1903*

*   *   *

'*There can be no other test of the credit of a country than the price at which it can borrow.*'

— *Commons, London. 2nd June 1908*

*   *   *

'*I am afraid I cannot give any explanation of the freaks of fortune in the world.*'

— *Commons, London. 20th April 1910*

*   *   *

'*We now know with accuracy the injury which has been done, at any rate to our finances. We meet this afternoon under the shadow of last year. It is not the time to bewail the past; it is the time to pay the bill. It is not for me to apportion the burden. I cannot present myself before the Committee in the guise of an impartial judge; I am only the public executioner.*'

— *Commons, London. 11th April 1927*

*   *   *

'*Every new administration, not excluding ourselves, arrives in power with bright and benevolent ideas of using public money to do good. The more frequent the changes of government, the more numerous are the bright ideas, and the more frequent the elections, the more benevolent they become.*'

— *Commons, London. 11th April 1927*

*   *   *

43

'*In the art of drafting (Income Tax Law) there seems to be a complete disdain of the full stop, and even the humble colon is an object to be avoided.*'

— *Commons, London. 19th April 1927*

*   *   *

'*It would be easy to give an epitome of the financial year which has closed. The road has lain continually uphill, the weather has been wet and cheerless, and the Lords Commissioners of His Majesty's Treasury have been increasingly uncheered by alcoholic stimulants.*'

— *Commons, London. 24th April 1928*

*   *   *

'*The detailed method of spending the money has not yet been fully thought out, but we are assured on the highest authority that if only enough resources and energy is used, there will be no difficulty in getting rid of the stuff.*

'*This is the policy which used to be stigmatised by the late Mr Thomas Gibson Bowles as the policy of buying a biscuit early in the morning and walking around all day looking for a dog to give it to.*'

— *Commons, London. 1929*

*   *   *

'*I must not say how much better we are than at the twenty-third month of the last war, nor how our output compares with the peak of the last war, because it is contended conditions have changed. This is rather easy money for the critics. A handful of Members can fill a couple of days' debate with disparaging charges against our war effort, and every ardent or disaffected section of the Press can take it up, and*

44

... rest on Hitler's chair outside the ruins
... the Fuhrer's air raid shelter in
...rlin at the end of World War II.
...e Russian officers in the foreground
...are the enjoyment of the scene.

...cknowledging the cheers of the Ayr,
...cotland, crowds after receiving the
...reedom of the Burgh; 15th May 1947.

With Lord Beaverbrook – 'The Beaver' – aboard HMS *Prince of Wales*.

Artist at work. Sir Winston painting above the little fishing village of Camara da Lobus, Funchal. The lady in the picture is Mrs C B Nairn, wife of the then British Consul in Madeira. 1950.

ost to Margaret, daughter of
dent Truman (*second from R*). Also
is group at Chartwell, 4th June
, are Mr and Mrs Walter Gifford
Mary (Churchill) and husband
stopher Soames.

val in Glasgow to address vast
vds at a Conservative Election
ting – with that old familiar
ting . . .

Churchill speaks, the
crowd roars: the Royal
Wanstead School Fête,
21st July 1951.

A beaming Winston at the
1952 christening of his
eighth grandchild,
Jeremy Soames, son of
daughter Mary. (Field
Marshal Montgomery was
godfather.)

the whole can cry a dismal cacophonous chorus of stinking fish all round the world.'

— *Commons, London. 29th July 1941*

*   *   *

In 1945 the Labour Party took over power from Churchill and one of the first changes they made was to substitute nickel for silver coinage. The following year Churchill made this scathing comment:

'*And now the British housewife, as she stands in the queues to buy her bread ration, will fumble in her pocket in vain for a silver sixpence. Under the Socialist Government, nickel will have to be good enough for her. In future, we shall still be able to say "every cloud has a nickel lining".*'

— *Blackpool. October 1946*

*   *   *

'*I do not believe that a successful export trade can be founded upon a starved home market.*'

— *Commons, London. 28th October 1947*

*   *   *

'*The word "disinflation" has been coined to avoid the unpopular term "deflation" . . . I suppose that presently when "disinflation" also wins its bad name, the Chancellor (Sir Stafford Cripps) will call it "non-undisinflation" and will start again.*'

— *Commons, London. 27th October 1949*

*   *   *

45

Commenting on the need for England to stand on her own economic feet, he said:

'We have no assurance that anyone is going to keep the British Lion as a pet.'

– Broadcast. December 1951

* * *

'A State Official or employee has only to keep his office hours punctually and do his best and if anything goes wrong he can send in the bill to the Chancellor of the Exchequer. He is truly what is called "disinterested" in the sense that he gains no advantage from wisdom and suffers no penalty for error.'

– Liverpool. 2nd October 1951

* * *

Mrs Mann (Labour):

'Is the Prime Minister aware that . . . the Mint has decided to issue the coins with "Elizabeth II", and Scots who object to this title are placed in an awful dilemma?'

The Prime Minister:

'I hope that theoretical refinements will not stop the normal conduct of business.'

* * *

Accused of spending valuable money on the direct importation of cigars from hard-currency areas, Churchill told MP's on his seventy-seventh birthday that:

'I have not for quite a long time imported any cigars from such areas.'

And added, with a smile: *'But I have received some from time to time.'*

– Commons, London.

On Politics and
Politicians

On Politics and Politicians

'*Politics are almost as exciting as war, and quite as dangerous. In war, you can only be killed once, but in politics many times.*

– 1920

*　　*　　*

'*It would be a great reform in politics if wisdom could be made to spread as easily and as rapidly as folly.*'

*　　*　　*

'*I have fought more elections than anyone here, and on the whole they are great fun. But there ought to be interludes of tolerance, hard work and study of social problems between them. Having rows for the sake of having rows between politicians might be good from time to time, but it is not a good habit of political life.*'

*　　*　　*

48

'*I will not pretend that, if I had to choose between Communism and Nazi-ism, I would choose Communism. I hope not to be called upon to survive in the world under a government of either of those dispensations.*'

— *Commons, London. 14th April 1937*

*　　*　　*

'*It is an error to believe that the world began when any particular party or statesman got into office. It has all been going on quite a long time.*'

*　　*　　*

'*The electors, based on universal suffrage, may do what they like, and afterwards they have to like what they do.*'

— *Blackpool. 5th October 1946*

*　　*　　*

'*Politics are very much like war; we may even have to use poison gas at times.*'

*　　*　　*

'*Well, one can always consult a man and ask him: "Would you like your head cut off tomorrow?" and after he has said: "I would rather not", cut it off. Consultation is a vague and elastic term.*'

— *Commons, London. 7th May 1947*

*　　*　　*

'*Just as eels get used to skinning, politicians get used to being caricatured.*'

*   *   *

Asked by a journalist to define the qualifications necessary to become a politician, Churchill said:

'*It is the ability to foretell what is going to happen tomorrow, next week, next month, and next year. And to have the ability afterwards to explain why it didn't happen.*'

*   *   *

'*Some men change their party for the sake of their principles; others their principles for the sake of their party.*'

*   *   *

Asked whether he would consider separating the Ministry of Agriculture from the Ministry of Fisheries, the Prime Minister said:

'*It would not, I feel, be a good arrangement to have a separate department for every industry of national importance. These two industries have for long been associated departmentally, and, after all, there are many ancient links between fish and chips.*'

*   *   *

On another matter concerning the Ministry of Agriculture he wrote this memorandum:

'*Have you done justice to rabbit production? Although rabbits are not by themselves nourishing, they are a pretty good mitigation of vegetarianism. They eat mainly grass and greenstuffs, so what is the harm in encouraging their multiplication in captivity?*'

*   *   *

'I am afraid that a large part of the object of every country is to throw the blame for an impending failure upon some other country while willing, if possible, to win the Nobel Peace Prize for itself.'

– Commons, London. 23rd November 1932

*　　*　　*

To a very ambitious Minister of Public Works:

'Do not let spacious plans for a new world divert your energies from saving what is left of the old.'

*　　*　　*

'If I valued the honourable gentleman's opinion, I might get angry.'

– January 1913

*　　*　　*

Churchill made many telling remarks about the House of Commons:

'There are two main characteristics of the House of Commons which will command the approval and the support of reflective and experienced members. They will, I have no doubt, sound odd to foreign ears.

The first is that its shape should be oblong and not semicircular. Here is a very potent factor of our political life. The semicircular assembly, which appeals to political theorists, enables every individual or every group to move round the centre, adopting various shades of pink according as the weather changes.'

– Commons, London. October 1943

*　　*　　*

Just before the new chamber of the House of Commons was due to be opened, replacing the one destroyed during the war, Churchill went on a tour of inspection. Entering the inner lobby, which was bathed in white fluorescent light, Churchill exclaimed:

'Good heavens! The Moscow Underground!'

— October 1950

*   *   *

'The Cabinet is the creature of the House of Commons. It springs from the House of Commons and dwells in the House of Commons. It is checked and corrected by the House of Commons, and by the shrug of the shoulder of the Private Members of the House the Cabinet can be scattered.'

— Commons, London. 16th February 1911

On Socialism
and Socialists

On Socialism and Socialists

'Socialism is the philosophy of failure, the creed of ignorance and the gospel of envy.'

*   *   *

'The inherent vice of capitalism is the unequal sharing of blessings. The inherent vice of socialism is the unequal sharing of miseries.'

– Commons, London. 22nd October 1945

*   *   *

'I deeply fear the doctrines and policies of the Socialist Government have destroyed, or are rapidly destroying, our national life. Nothing they can plan and order and rush around enforcing will take its place. They have broken the mainspring and until we get a new one the watch will not go.'

– Commons, London. 28th October 1947

*   *   *

His opinion of the Chamberlain government in 1937 was:
  '*They are decided only to be undecided, resolved to be irresolute, adamant for drift, all-powerful for impotency.*'

*   *   *

When Hugh Gaitskell was Labour Party Minister of Fuel and Power in 1947, he campaigned to have fewer baths as a way of saving coal:
  '*I have never had a great many baths myself, and I can assure those who have them as a habit that it does not make much difference to their health if they have fewer.*' he said in his speech.
Churchill, of course, could not let this suggestion go without comment:
  '*When Ministers of the Crown speak like this on behalf of His Majesty's Government*', he said, '*the Prime Minister and his friends have no need to wonder why they are getting increasingly into bad odour.*'
                                        – Commons, London. October 1947

*   *   *

Of Health Minister, Aneurin Bevan, whom Churchill nicknamed Britain's 'Minister of Disease', he said:
  '*I have no doubt that the highest exponents in the medical profession would concur that a period of prolonged seclusion and relief from any responsible duties would be an equal benefit to Mr. Bevan and to the National Health Service.*'
                                        – July 1948

*   *   *

Just after the Second World War, the Attlee government proposed to introduce so much legislation that MPs were extremely hard-worked. By August, many MP's, particularly Socialists, pressed Herbert Morrison, the Deputy Prime Minister, to say when the Parliamentary recess would begin. Churchill rose to comment:

'We are all anxious for the Labour Members to get away in time for the grouse-shooting.'

* * *

'I hope you have all mastered the official Socialist jargon, which our masters, as they call themselves, wish us to learn.

You must not use the word poor, they are described as the "lower income group".

When it comes to a question of freezing a workman's wages, the Chancellor of the Exchequer speaks of "arresting increases in personal income". The idea is that formerly income tax payers used to be well-to-do and that, therefore, it will be popular and safe to hit at them. Sir Stafford Cripps does not like to mention the word "wages" but that is what he means.

There is a lovely one about houses and homes. They are in the future to be called "accommodation units". I don't know how we are to sing our old song "Home, Sweet Home". "Accommodation Unit, Sweet Accommodation Unit, there's no place like our Accommodation Unit".'

– Cardiff, February 1950

* * *

'*The difference between our outlook (the Conservatives) and the Socialist outlook on life is the difference between the ladder and the queue.*

We are for the ladder. Let all try their best to climb. They are for the queue. Let each wait in his place till his turn comes. But we ask: "What happens if anyone slips out of his place in the queue?"

"Ah," say the Socialists, "our officials – and we have plenty of them – come and put him back in it, or perhaps put him lower down to teach others."

And when they come back to us and say: "We have told you what happens when anyone slips out of the queue, but what is your answer to what happens if anyone slips off the ladder?"

Our reply is: "We shall have a good net and the finest social ambulance service in the world".'

– *Party Political Broadcast. October 1951*

On Other Nations

On Other Nations

'There is not one single social or economic principle or concept in the philosophy of the Russian Bolshevik which has not been realised, carried into action, and enshrined in immutable laws a million years ago by the white ant.'

*   *   *

'Russia is a riddle wrapped in a mystery inside an enigma.'
— BBC Broadcast. 1st October 1939

*   *   *

'Let there be sunshine on both sides of the Iron Curtain; and if ever the sunshine be equal on both sides, the Curtain will be no more.'

*   *   *

Marshal Montgomery (*second R*) and General Eisenhower (*R*) with
ston at the El Alamein Reunion, London; 19th October 1951. (Presenting
igar is stage producer Ralph Reader.)

Chancellor of Bristol University. 14th December 1951.

President Truman and Churchill with a painting of US Frigate *Constitution* firing on HMS *Java* in the 1812 War. Aboard the Presidential Yacht; 6th January 1952.

Embarking for the United States, with his son-in-law Christopher Soames. 30th December 1952.

Turkish Premier Adnan Menderes, in London, 14th October 1952, enjoys a Churchill story.

Prince Philip, Duke of Edinburgh, with General Matthew B Ridgeway, then Supreme Commander, Allied Powers in Europe, and Sir Winston at The Pilgrims' Dinner. Savoy Hotel, London, 1952.

Two farewells . . .

(*L*) to Ethiopian Emperor Haile Selassie, after lunch at 10 Downing Street, 22nd October 1954.

(*B*) to President Eisenhower after a visit to The White House, 29th June 1954.

In lively discussion with King Gustav of Sweden, shortly after Sir Winston's Nobel Prize Award for Literature; 11th November 1953.

Told of the new creed that children were being taught in Russia:
'*I love Lenin,*
Lenin was poor, therefore I love poverty,
Lenin went hungry, therefore I can go hungry,
Lenin was often cold, therefore I shall not ask for warmth'
Churchill said, caustically:
'*Christianity with a tomahawk!*'

*　　　*　　　*

'*I am by no means sure that China will remain for generations in the Communist grip. The Chinese said of themselves several thousand years ago: "China is a sea that salts all the waters that flow into it".*

There is another Chinese saying about their country which dates from the fourth century: "The tail of China is large and will not be wagged".

I like that one. The British democracy approves the principle of movable heads and unwaggable national tails.'

– United States Congress, Washington. January 1952

*　　　*　　　*

'*India is an abstraction! India is no more a political personality than Europe. India is a geographical term. It is no more a united nation than the Equator.*'

*　　　*　　　*

'*One voyage to India is enough; the others are merely repetition.*'

*　　　*　　　*

'*There is only one thing worse than fighting with allies, and that is fighting without them.*'

*　　*　　*

On the subject of neutral nations, Churchill had this to say during the early days of the Second World War:

'*Each one of them hopes that if he feeds the crocodile enough, the crocodile will eat him last.*'

*　　*　　*

'*The Almighty in His infinite wisdom did not see fit to create Frenchmen in the image of Englishmen.*'

*　　*　　*

Churchill described Paris just after the First World War as:

'*A terrible society, grimly polished and trellised with live wires.*'

*　　*　　*

'*We shall continue to operate on the Italian donkey at both ends – with a carrot and with a stick.*'

– May 1943

*　　*　　*

'*The American chicken is a small bird compared with the standard English fowl. Attractively served with rice and auxiliaries of all kinds, he makes an excellent dish. Still, I am on the side of the big chicken as* regularly as Providence is on that of the big battalions. Indeed it seems strange in so large a country to find such small chickens. Conscious, perhaps, of their inferiority, the inhabitants call them "squabs". What an insulting title for a capon.'

– 1933

*   *   *

'A dangerous, yet almost universal, habit of the American people is the drinking of immense quantities of iced water. This has become a ritual. If you go into a cafeteria or drug-store and order a cup of coffee, a tumbler of iced water is immediately set before you. The bleak beverage is provided on every possible occasion: whatever you order, the man behind the counter will supply this apparently indispensable concomitant.'

– 1933

*   *   *

'Nor should it be supposed as you would imagine, to read some of the left-wing newspapers, that all Americans are multi-millionaires of Wall Street.

If they were all multi-millionaires, that would be no reason for condemning a system which has produced such material results.'
– Royal Albert Hall, London. April 1948

*   *   *

'I feel greatly honoured that you should have invited me to enter the United States Senate chamber and address the Representatives of both sides of Congress.

63

The fact that my American forebears have for so many generations played their part in the life of the United States, and that here I am, an Englishman, welcomed in your midst, makes this experience one of the most moving and thrilling of my life, which is already long and has not been entirely uneventful.

I wish indeed that my mother, whose memory I cherish across the vale of years, could have been here to see. By the way, I cannot help reflecting that if my father had been American and my mother British, instead of the other way round, I might have gotten here on my own.

In that case, this would not have been the first time you would have heard my voice. In that case, I should not have needed any invitation, but if I had it is hardly likely it would have been unanimous.

So perhaps things are better as they are. I may confess, however, that I do not feel quite like a fish out of water in a legislative assembly where English is spoken.'

– United States Congress, Washington. 26th December 1941

*   *   *

'The United States is a land of free speech; nowhere is speech freer, not even here where we sedulously cultivate it even in its most repulsive forms.

But when I see some of the accounts of conversations that I am supposed to have had with the President of the United States, I can only recall a Balfourian phrase at which I laughed many years ago, when he said that the accounts which were given bore no more relation to the actual facts than the wildest tales of the Arabian Nights do to the ordinary incidents of the domestic life in the East.'

– Commons, London. September 1944

*   *   *

'*It cannot be in the interest of Russia to go on irritating the United States. There are no people in the world who are so slow to develop hostile feelings against a foreign country as the Americans, and there are no people who, once estranged, are more difficult to win back. The American eagle sits on his perch, a large, strong bird with a formidable beak and claws. There he sits motionless, and Mr Gromyko is sent day after day to prod him with a sharp pointed stick – now his neck, now under his wings, now his tail feathers. All the time the eagle keeps still. But it would be a great mistake to suppose that nothing is going on inside the breast of the eagle.*'

– Commons, London. 5th June 1946

*　　*　　*

'*We must be very careful nowadays – I perhaps all the more, because of my American forebears – in what we say about the American Constitution. I will, therefore, content myself with the observation that no Constitution was written in better English.*'

– Coronation Luncheon, Westminster Hall. London. 27th May 1953

*　　*　　*

In 1954, when world tensions were at a peak, it was suggested by a Labour Party member that Churchill should arrange a top level meeting between representatives of the United States, the Soviet Union and Great Britain to alleviate the situation. His reaction was to say:

'*Perhaps on this somewhat delicate topic I may be permitted by the House to take refuge in metaphor. Many anxieties have been expressed*

65

recently at the severe character of the course of the Grand National Steeplechase, but I am sure that it could not be improved by asking the horses to try to jump two fences at the same time.'

*　　*　　*

His reaction to New York City was once expressed in seven words:

'Newspapers too thick, lavatory paper too thin.'

On Democracy

On Democracy

'*Democracy is the occasional necessity of deferring to the opinions of other people.*'

*　　*　　*

'*The prerogatives of the Crown have become the privileges of the people.*'

– *Harrow. 1st December 1944*

*　　*　　*

'*Many forms of government have been tried and will be tried in this world of sin and woe. No one pretends that democracy is perfect or all-wise.*

Indeed, it has been said that democracy is the worst form of government except all those other forms that have been tried from time to time.'

– *Commons, London. November 1947*

*　　*　　*

'*We welcome any country where the people own the government, and not the government the people.*'
> – *The Hague. 7th May 1948*

*   *   *

'*Free speech carries with it the evil of all foolish, unpleasant and venomous things that are said but, on the whole, we would rather lump them than do away with them.*'
> – *Commons, London. July 1952*

On Dictators

On Dictators

'The dictator in all his pride is held in the grip of his Party machine. He can go forward – he cannot go back. He must blood his hounds and show them sport, or else, like Actaeon of old, be devoured by them. All-strong without, he is all-weak within.'

– London. 16th October 1938

* * *

'Dictators ride to and fro upon tigers which they dare not dismount. And the tigers are getting hungry.'

* * *

'Hitler has told us that it was a crime in such circumstances on our part to go to the aid of the Greeks. I do not wish to enter into argument with experts.'

– Commons, London. 7th May 1941

* * *

72

'*Hitler made a contract with the demon of the air, but the contract ran out before the job was done, and the demon has taken on an engagement with the rival firm.*'

– Commons, London. 2nd July 1942

*   *   *

On Hitler and Mussolini:

'*You see these dictators on their pedestals, surrounded by the bayonets of their soldiers and the truncheons of their police . . . yet in their hearts there is unspoken, unspeakable fear.*

A little mouse, a little tiny mouse of thought, appears in the room and even the mightiest potentates are thrown into panic.'

*   *   *

'*Into that void strode a maniac of ferocious genius – the expression of the most virulent hatred that has ever corroded the human breast . . . Corporal Hitler.*'

*   *   *

'*Hitler, in one of his recent discourses, declared that the fight was between those who have been through the Adolf Hitler schools and those who have been at Eton. Hitler has forgotten Harrow!*'

*   *   *

'*When Herr Hitler escaped his bomb on 20th July, he described his survival as providential. I think that from a purely military point of view, we can all agree with him for certainly it would be most unfortunate if the Allies were to be deprived, in the closing phases of the struggle, of that form of warlike genius by which Corporal Schickelgruber has so notably contributed to our victory.*'

*   *   *

'*As a freeborn Englishman, what I hate is the sense of being at any-body's mercy or anybody's power, be it Hitler or Attlee. We are approach-ing very near to dictatorship in this country, dictatorship, that is to say –
I will be quite candid with the House – without either its criminality or its efficiency.*'

– *Commons, London. 11th November 1947*

*   *   *

'*One of the disadvantages of dictatorship is that the dictator is often dictated to by others – and what he did to others may often be done back again to him.*'

– *Commons, London. 11th May 1953*

On Arms and
the Armed Forces

On Arms and the Armed Forces

Talking about disarmament among nations in 1928, Churchill said:

'Once upon a time, all the animals in the zoos decided that they would disarm, and they arranged to have a conference to arrange the matter. So the rhinoceros said, when he opened the proceedings, that the use of teeth was barbarous and horrible and ought to be strictly prohibited by general consent. Horns, which were mainly defensive weapons, would of course, have to be allowed.

The buffalo, the stag, the porcupine and even the little hedgehog, all said they would vote with the rhino. But the lion and tiger took a different view. They defended teeth, and even claws, which they described as honourable weapons of immortal antiquity. The panther, the leopard, the puma and the whole tribe of small cats all supported the lion and the tiger.

Then the bear spoke. He proposed that both teeth and horns should be banned and never used again for fighting by any animal. It would be quite enough if animals were allowed to give each other a good hug

en Elizabeth and Prince Philip leave 'Number Ten' after a dinner party; 4th April 1955.

statesman poses with the Mayor of Hastings after being presented with a
trait of himself from the Cinque Ports and associated towns.

The statesman is visited at his Chartwell home by seven proud officers and forty equally proud other ranks of the 5th (Cinque Ports) Battalion of The Royal Sussex Regiment, TA. Lady Churchill is seen in the background with three of her grandchildren. Kent, April 1956.

Sir Anthony Eden, then the British Prime Minister, receives his mentor, Winston Churchill, at No. 10 Downing Street. London, November 1956.

Sir Winston goes in to receive The Charlemagne Prize for his services to Western Europe. Aachen, May 1956.

Winston arrives in Nice . . . and, unexpectedly, pouring rain!
March 1959.

(*Above*) April 1959, the French Riviera. Sir Winston
enjoys a visit to his neighbour, Somerset Maugham.

(*Left*) October 1959, Woodford. Sir Winston stops in his
election campaign to greet a famous constituent, tennis star
Christine Truman.

Sir Winston and Lady Churchill, Harrow School Speech Day;
16th November 1961.

Sir Winston greets the American Ambassador to London, Mr David Bruce, after
receiving his American passport on being made an honorary citizen of the
United States. London, April 1963.

when they quarrelled. No one could object to that. It was so fraternal and that would be a great step towards peace. However, all the other animals were very offended with the bear, and the turkey fell into a perfect panic.

The discussion got so hot and angry that all those animals began thinking so much about horns and teeth and hugging when they argued about the peaceful intentions that had brought them together, that they began to look at one another in a very nasty way.

Luckily, the keepers were able to calm them to go back quietly to their cages and they began to feel quite friendly with one another again.'

*　　　*　　　*

'False ideas have been spread about the country that disarmament means peace.'

– Commons, London. 14th March 1934

*　　　*　　　*

'I cannot believe that, after armaments in all countries have reached a towering height, they will settle down and continue at a hideous level.'

– Commons, London. 23rd April 1936

*　　　*　　　*

'It is remarkable and indeed odd that the more efficient fire-arms have become, the fewer people are killed by them. The explanation of this apparent paradox is simply that human beings are much more ingenious in getting out of the way of missiles which are fired at them than they are at improving the direction and guidance of these individual missiles.'

– Commons, London. 1st February 1954

*　　　*　　　*

'*The argument is now put forward that we must never use the atomic bomb until, or unless, it has been used against us first. In other words, you must never fire until you have been shot dead. That seems to me a silly thing to say.*'

*　　*　　*

Talking about the pistol he often carried, Churchill remarked to his bodyguard:

'*You see, Thompson, they will never take me alive. I will always get one or two before they can shoot me down.*'

*　　*　　*

'*We have never been likely to get into trouble by having an extra thousand or two of up-to-date airplanes at our disposal.*

As the man whose mother-in-law had died in Brazil replied when asked how the remains should be disposed of: "Embalm, cremate and bury. Take no chances".'

– April 1938

*　　*　　*

'*It is true that, as against a civilised foe, it is most undesirable that the dum-dum bullet should be used, and I believe that in the early days of the South African War a good deal of inconvenience was caused by the fact that the ammunition had to be changed.*'

– Commons, London. 19th July 1906

*　　*　　*

'*This tank, the A22, was ordered off the drawing board and large numbers went into production very quickly. As might be expected, it had many defects and teething troubles and when these became apparent the tank was appropriately christened,* The Churchill.'
— *Commons, London. July 1942*

* * *

Irate because a new kind of bomb had been delayed in manufacture, Churchill sent this memorandum to General Ismay:
'*Any chortling by officials who have been slothful in pushing this bomb will be viewed with great disfavour by me.*'
— *During the Second World War*

* * *

When asked who had supplied the North Koreans with so many jet planes, Churchill said:
'*Although there are movements ever being made in aerial locomotion, it would be premature to suppose that they came from the moon.*'
— *During the Korean conflict. May 1952*

* * *

'*One of the most remarkable features of the British army for a great number of years had been its number of generals.*'
— *Commons, London. 24th February 1903*

* * *

In a conversation with Lord Onslow, Churchill asked how a particular platoon had fared. When he learned that everyone had been taken prisoner, Churchill remarked:

'*Taken prisoner? What you mean, young man, is: "herded into captivity by inefficient generals".*'

*   *   *

The conversation continued and Lord Onslow was asked to give an account of conditions at the front from which he had just returned. When Onslow had finished, Churchill turned to the generals present and commented:

'*I have listened to this young officer with great interest. Only those who have been in the frying pan are really qualified to talk about the heat.*'

             – Cairo, during the Second World War

*   *   *

A pompous assumption from a general during the Second World War that 'putting the troops in the picture before a battle was the sort of familiarity which breeds contempt', caused Churchill to say:

'*You know, general, without a certain amount of familiarity it is extraordinarily difficult to breed anything at all.*'

*   *   *

'*I remember it was the fashion in the army when a court-martial was being held and the prisoner was brought in, that he should be asked if he objected to being tried by the president or to any of those officers*

who composed the court-martial. *One occasion a prisoner was so insubordinate as to answer: "I object to the whole . . . lot of you".'*
— Commons, London. *9th February 1927*

*　　*　　*

In his campaign to establish a Minister of Supply to help prepare against the threat of a second World War, Churchill said:

'*A friend of mine, the other day, saw a number of persons engaged in peculiar evolutions, genuflections and gestures. He wondered whether it was some novel form of gymnastics or a new religion or whether they were a party of lunatics out for an airing.*

They were a searchlight company of London Territorials who were doing their exercises as well as they could without having a searchlight!'

*　　*　　*

In response to a complaint from an officer that the Navy was not being allowed to play its traditional role in the war, Churchill retorted:

'*Well, Admiral, have you ever asked yourself what the traditions of the Royal Navy are? I will tell you in three words. Rum, sodomy and the lash!*'

*　　*　　*

'*Will you kindly explain to me the reasons which debar individuals in certain branches from rising by merit to commissioned rank? If a cook may rise, or a steward, why not an electrical artificer or an ordnance man? If a telegraphist may rise, why not a painter? Apparently, there is no difficulty about painters rising in Germany.*'
— *Note to the Second Sea Lord. 1939*

*　　*　　*

'*We must be very careful not to assign to this deliverance the attributes of victory. Wars are not won by evacuations. But there was a victory inside this deliverance, which should be noted. It was gained by the Air Force.*'

– Commons, London, on Dunkirk. *4th June 1940*

*   *   *

'*I entirely agree that civil authority has supreme authority over the military men.*'

*   *   *

'*I admire men who stand up for their country in defeat, even though I am on the other side.*'

On Invasion

On Invasion

In 1943 Churchill decided that church bells would no longer be reserved for use as a warning in case of invasion. When asked about a substitute warning signal, he replied:

'Replacement does not arise. I cannot help thinking that anything like a serious invasion would be bound to leak out.'

* * *

General 'Pug' Ismay, Churchill's wartime Chief of Staff, recalls one late-night discussion by the Defence Committee on the exact timing of the D-day landings:

'I regret to admit that I was half asleep when I heard the Prime Minister ask when William the Conqueror had landed. Here was my chance. "1066!", I exclaimed. To my surprise this was greeted with a roar of laughter, and the Prime Minister said pityingly: "Pug, you should have been in your basket ages ago".'

* * *

That Britain should prepare only for a defensive war was a suggestion Churchill couldn't tolerate:

'I cannot subscribe to the idea that it might be possible to dig ourselves in and make no preparations for anything other than passive defence. It is the theory of the turtle, which is disproved at every Lord Mayor's Banquet.'

*   *   *

'The intervention which I make is without precedent and the reason for that intervention is also without precedent, and the fact that the reason for my intervention is without precedent is the reason why I must ask for a precedent for my intervention.'

– Commons, London. November 1941

*   *   *

On the threatened German occupation of London:

'If they come to London I shall take a rifle – I'm not a bad shot – I will put myself in a pill-box at the bottom of Downing Street, and shoot till I have no more ammunition, and then they can damn well shoot me.'

*   *   *

Britain declared war upon Japan in 1941, and Churchill wrote to the Japanese Ambassador in London advising him of this. The note was very formal and Churchill commented:

'Some people do not like this ceremonial style. But when you have to kill a man it costs nothing to be polite.'

*   *   *

85

During a war-time broadcast in 1940:

'We are waiting for Hitler's long-promised invasion. So are the fishes.'

*   *   *

On the German invasion of Russia in 1942:

'There is a winter, you know, in Russia. Hitler forgot about this. He must have been very loosely educated. We all heard about it at school, but he forgot it. I have never made such a bad mistake as that.'

*   *   *

In answer to the French Generals who asked him how England would withstand an invasion:

'I said that of course I was not a military expert and I was always very careful in not meddling in these sort of questions, but that my professional advisers told me that the best way to deal with such an invasion would be to drown as many as possible on the way over, and knock the rest on the head as they crawled ashore.'

*   *   *

In a speech to the US Congress on the Japanese attack on Pearl Harbour:

'They have certainly embarked upon a very considerable undertaking.'

*   *   *

'If Hitler invaded Hell I would make at least a favourable reference to the Devil in the House of Commons.'

*   *   *

Churchill described Hitler's attack on Russia in 1942 as:

'*I see advancing in hideous onslaught the Nazi war-machine, with its clanking, heel-clicking, dandified Prussian officers, its crafty expert agents fresh from the cowing and tying down of a dozen countries. I see also the dull, drilled, docile, brutish masses of the Hun soldiery plodding on like a swarm of crawling locusts . . . they have, of course, the consolation of knowing that they are being led not by the German General Staff but by Corporal Hitler himself.*'

*   *   *

Abusing Mussolini for asking Hitler for more troops to complete the attack on Greece, Churchill said:

'*Here surely is the world's record in the domain of the ridiculous and the contemptible. This whipped jackal, Mussolini, who to save his own skin has made all Italy a vassal state of Hitler's Empire, comes frisking up to the side of the German tiger with yelpings, not only of appetite – that could be understood – but even of triumph.*'

*   *   *

'*The Battle of Egypt is not the end, it is not even the beginning of the end, it is perhaps the end of the beginning.*'

*   *   *

'*The events in Libya are only part of the story. They are only part of the story of the decline and fall of the Italian Empire, that will not take a future Gibbon so long to write as the original work.*'

– *London. February 1941*

*   *   *

He described Britain's attitude towards the Turks in 1943 as:

'We must start by treating them purry-purry, puss-puss, then later we shall harden!'

*   *   *

Amazed at how little affected those countries under Nazi tyranny had been, Churchill commented:

'We are surrounded by fat cattle lying in luscious pastures with their paws crossed.'

*   *   *

During the Allied invasion of Italy when an attempt to establish the Anzio bridgehead was made, he said:

'We hoped to land a wild-cat that would tear out the bowels of the Boche. Instead we have stranded a vast whale with its tail flopping about in the water.'

*   *   *

When the Americans wanted to sack the King of Italy and Badoglio in 1944, he said:

'Why break the handle of the coffee-pot at this stage and burn your fingers trying to hold it? Why not wait till we get to Rome and let it cool off?'

On War

On War

'War is a game with a good deal of chance in it, and, from the little I have seen of it, I should say that nothing in war ever goes right, except by accident.'

*　　*　　*

'As it is, those who can win a war well can rarely make good peace, and those who could make a good peace would never have won the war.'

*　　*　　*

'No one can guarantee success in war, but only deserve it.'

*　　*　　*

'Any clever person can make plans for winning a war if he has no responsibility for carrying them out.'

*　　*　　*

'*In war you don't have to be nice: you only have to be right.*'

*   *   *

'*Great quarrels, it has been said, often arise from small occasions but never from small causes.*'

*   *   *

'*Wars are not won by heroic militias.*'

*   *   *

'*At the beginning of this war, megalomania was the only form of sanity.*'
> – Commons, London. November 1915

*   *   *

Asked if he found it hard to sleep during the war, Churchill said:
'*Difficult? Oh no, I just put my head on the pillow, said damn everybody and went off.*'

*   *   *

'*If the capacity of a War Minister may be measured in any way by the amount of money he can obtain from his colleagues for military purposes, the right honourable Gentleman will most certainly go down in history as the greatest War Minister this country has ever had.*'
> – Commons, London. 13th May 1901

*   *   *

'*When millions of people are lacerated and inflamed against each other by reciprocal injuries, some element of outside aid and even of outside pressure is indispensable.*'

– Commons, London. 14th April 1937

*   *   *

To Brendan Bracken, MP:
'*You know, you have got to hand it to Hitler. The war has been on only a few minutes and here is an air raid already.*'

*   *   *

Talking about the Blitz, Churchill made these remarks:
'*Statisticians may amuse themselves by calculating that after making allowance for the working of the law of diminishing returns, it would take ten years, at the present rate, for half of the houses of London to be demolished. After that, of course, progress would be much slower.*'

– October 1940

*   *   *

In a wartime memorandum to the Minister of Food, Churchill discussed ice-cream and whether its manufacture should be prohibited:
'*I cannot judge whether the destruction of this amenity is worthwhile. I suppose the large numbers of American troops in this country will have their own arrangements made for them. They are great addicts of ice-cream, which is said to be a rival to alcoholic drinks.*'

*   *   *

'*Nothing is more dangerous in wartime than to live in the temperamental atmosphere of a Gallup Poll, always feeling one's pulse and taking one's temperature.*

I see it said that leaders should keep their ears to the ground. All I can say is that the British nation will find it very hard to look up to the leaders who are detected in that somewhat ungainly posture.'
— *Commons, London. September 1941*

*   *   *

'*Fanned by the fierce winds of war, medical science and surgical art have advanced unceasingly, hand in hand. There has certainly been no lack of subjects for treatment. The medical profession at least cannot complain of unemployment through lack of raw material.*'
— *Guildhall, London. 10th September 1947*

*   *   *

Writing retrospectively about the Second World War, Churchill said:
'*When I look back on all these worries, I remember the story of the old man who said that he had had a lot of trouble in his life . . . most of which never happened.*'

93

On Diplomacy

On Diplomacy

'*The reason for having diplomatic relations is not to confer a compliment – but to secure a convenience.*'

– *Commons, London. 17th November 1949*

*   *   *

'*The zeal and efficiency of a diplomatic representative is measured by the quality and not the quantity of the information he supplies.*'

*   *   *

'*Trying to maintain good relations with the Communists is like wooing a crocodile. You do not know whether to tickle it under the chin or beat it over the head. When it opens its mouth you cannot tell whether it is trying to smile or preparing to eat you up.*'

*   *   *

A Cabinet colleague was rather unnecessarily trying to impress Churchill on the wisdom of strengthening the bonds of friendship with the Americans in the mid-war period. Rather excitedly he exclaimed:

'*We must give them the kiss of friendship!*'

Churchill looked at him somewhat sourly and replied:

'*Yes. Of course. But not on both cheeks.*'

*   *   *

'*I make it a rule, as far as I possibly can, to say nothing in this House upon matters which I am not sure are already known to the General Staffs of foreign countries.*'

     – *Commons, London. 12th November 1936*

*   *   *

'*It is a very fine thing to refuse an invitation, but it is a good thing to wait till you get it first.*'

     – *London, February 1911*

*   *   *

'*I insist that I be the host at dinner tomorrow evening. I think I have one or two claims to precedence. To begin with, I come first in seniority and alphabetically. In the second place, I represent the longest established of the three governments. And in the third place, tomorrow happens to be my birthday.*'

     – *Diplomatic conference, Teheran. 1943*

*   *   *

'*When I am abroad, I always make it a rule never to criticise or attack the government of my own country. I make up for lost time when I come home.*'

— *Commons, London. April, 1947*

*   *   *

Shortly after Churchill was defeated in 1949 he was offered the Order of the Garter. He turned it down, saying:

'*Why should I accept the Order of the Garter from His Majesty, when the people have just given me the Order of the Boot?*'

On Truth

On Truth

'The truth is incontrovertible. Panic may resent it; ignorance may deride it; malice may distort it, but there it is.'

*   *   *

'I am reminded of the remark of the witty Irishman who said: "There are a terrible lot of lies going about the world, and the worst of it is that half of them are true".'

– February 1906

*   *   *

'In wartime, truth is so precious that she should always be attended by a bodyguard of lies.'

*   *   *

'It is a fine thing to be honest, but it is also very important to be right.'

*   *   *

'*The honourable member is never lucky in the coincidence of his facts with the truth.*'

– *Commons, London. July 1954*

*   *   *

'*I like the martial and commanding air with which the right honourable Gentleman treats facts. He stands no nonsense from them.*'

– *Commons, London. 19th February 1909*

*   *   *

Squashing a question put by Mr Aneurin Bevan in the Commons, Churchill said mildly:

'*I should think it hardly possible to state the opposite of the truth with more precision.*'

*   *   *

'*You must look at facts because they look at you.*'

– *Commons, London. 7th May 1925*

*   *   *

'*It is no good the right honourable Gentleman (Ramsay MacDonald) shaking his head. He cannot shake away the facts.*'

– *Commons, London. 27th September 1926*

*   *   *

'*If there are any suspicions or insinuations to ventilate, here is the place, and now is the time. Full notice has been given, the place is privileged, and the time is extremely convenient.*'

– *Commons, London. 17th July 1913*

*   *   *

'*A balloon goes up quite easily for a certain distance, but after a certain distance it refuses to go up any farther, because the air is too rarefied to float it and sustain it. And, therefore, I would say, let us examine the concrete facts.*'

– St Andrews Hall, Glasgow. 11th October 1906

* * *

'*There was something rather hypocritical about tactics which tried to parade the claims of the children as an excuse for the acts of the parents.*'

– Commons, London. 1st May 1903

On Words

On Words

'*Short words are best and the old words when short are best of all.*'

*   *   *

'*Personally I like short words and vulgar fractions.*'
– Margate. October 1953

*   *   *

One of Churchill's greatest loves was books. He wrote of them:
'*If you cannot read all your books, at any rate handle, or, as it were,
fondle them – peer into them, let them fall open where they will, read
from the first sentence that arrests the eye, set them back on their shelves
with your own hands, arrange them on your own plan so that if you do
not know what is in them, you at least know where they are. Let them
be your friends; let them at any rate be your acquaintances.*'

*   *   *

'*There is a great deal of difference between the tired man who wants a book to read and the alert man who wants to read a book.*'

*   *   *

Churchill once squashed a bothersome author, who had asked whether he had read his latest book, by saying:
'*No, I only read for pleasure or profit.*'

*   *   *

Describing the development of his own early writing, he said:
'*I affected a combination of the styles of Macaulay and Gibbon, the staccato antithesis of the former, and the rolling sentences and genitival endings of the latter; and I stuck a bit in of my own from time to time.*'

*   *   *

'*Writing a book is an adventure. To begin with it is a toy and an amusement. Then it becomes a mistress, then it becomes a master, then it becomes a tyrant. The last phase is that just as you are about to be reconciled to your servitude, you kill the monster, and fling him about to the public.*'

*   *   *

'*There is a good saying to the effect that when a new book appears one should read an old one. As an author, I would not recommend too strict an adherence to this saying.*'

*   *   *

'*Certainly I have been fully qualified as far as the writing of books about wars is concerned; in fact, already in 1900 I could boast to have written as many books as Moses, and I have not stopped writing them since, except when momentarily interrupted by war, in all the intervening period.*'

*   *   *

'*For my part*', he announced in 1948, '*I consider that it will be found much better by all parties to leave the past to history, especially as I propose to write that history myself.*'

*   *   *

In 1953 Churchill was awarded the Nobel Prize for Literature. When he received notification of this, he said:

'*I notice that the first Englishman to receive the Nobel Prize was Rudyard Kipling and that another equally rewarded was Mr Bernard Shaw. I certainly cannot attempt to compete with either of these.*

I knew them quite well and my thought was much more in accord with Mr Rudyard Kipling than with Mr Bernard Shaw.

On the other hand, Mr Rudyard Kipling never thought much of me, whereas Mr Bernard Shaw often expressed himself in most flattering terms.'

*   *   *

George Bernard Shaw did not always approve of the Prime Minister's actions. On one occasion, the playwright sent Churchill two tickets to his new play with the invitation:

'*And bring a friend, if you have one.*'

Churchill replied that he was unable to attend on the opening night but that Shaw should send him two seats for the second performance. He added ' . . . *if there is one.*'

*   *   *

'*I have been a journalist and half my lifetime I have earned my living by selling words and, I hope, thoughts.*'
– Ottawa, Canada. January 1952

*   *   *

'*During my life I have often had to eat my own words and I have found them a wholesome diet.*'

*   *   *

'*I think "No comment" is a splendid expression. I am using it again and again. I got it from Sumner Welles.*'
– Washington. February 1946

*   *   *

'*I must say that this class of criticism which I read in the newspapers when I arrived on Sunday morning reminds me of the simple tale about the sailor who jumped into a dock – I think it was at Plymouth – to rescue a small boy from drowning.*

About a week later, this sailor was accosted by a woman who asked: "Are you the man who picked my son out of the dock the other night?"

The sailor replied modestly: "That is true, ma'am."

"Ah", replied the woman, "You are the man I am looking for . . . where is his cap?" '

*   *   *

Due to a fuel crisis just after the war, publication of some news-papers and periodicals was curtailed. One such affected was the *Spectator*. Its editor, Wilson Harris MP, in expressing his annoy-ance to Churchill, said:

'*The greatest intellectual weekly in Britain cannot come out for two weeks owing to Mr Shinwell's fuel crisis!*'

Churchill pretended not to hear, and then asked in a voice which his friends knew meant trouble:

'*What do you say is going to happen because of Shinwell?*'

Harris reiterated at great length, saying finally:

'. . . *and the* Spectator, *after a hundred years of continuous publication, will not appear next week or the next.*'

Churchill, who had been scowling throughout, suddenly smiled:

'*I am so glad,*' he said, with a wave of his cigar.

*　　*　　*

'*The Press is easier squashed than squared.*'

*　　*　　*

In 1899, Churchill discovered that there was another well-known Winston Churchill – an American novelist. He sent his namesake the following letter:

'*Mr Winston Churchill presents his compliments to Mr Winston Churchill, and begs to draw his attention to a matter which concerns them both. He has learnt from the press notices that Mr Winston Churchill proposes to bring out another novel entitled* Richard Carvel *which is certain to have a considerable sale both in England and America. Mr Winston Churchill is also the author of a novel now being published in serial form in* Macmillan's Magazine, *and for which he anticipates some sale in both England and America . . . He has no doubt that*

Mr Winston Churchill will recognise from this letter – if indeed by no other means – that there is grave danger of his works being mistaken for those of Mr Winston Churchill. He feels sure that Mr Winston Churchill desires this as little as he does himself. In future to avoid mistakes as far as possible, Mr Winston Churchill has decided to sign all published articles, stories, or other works "Winston Spencer Churchill", and not " Winston Churchill" as formerly.

He trusts that this arrangement will commend itself to Mr Winston Churchill . . . He takes this occasion of complimenting Mr Winston Churchill on the style and success of his works, which are always brought to his notice, whether in magazine or book form, and he trusts that Mr Winston Churchill has derived equal pleasure from any work of his that may have attracted his attention.'

*   *   *

In 1926, during the General Strike, Churchill was editor of the Government-sponsored newspaper the *British Gazette*. It was the only newspaper published at the time, and it was most unpopular with the workers because of its aggressive anti-strike content.

During a debate in the Commons, some months after the strike had ended, Churchill suddenly paused in the middle of a heated speech and glared fiercely at the Socialist benches:

'*I warn you,*' he said to his fearfully hushed audience, '*I warn you that if ever there is another general strike . . . we will let loose on you another* British Gazette.'

*   *   *

This story was told by Jan Christian Smuts, the former South African Premier, at a White House, Washington, dinner in 1946:

'*During the Boer War, Churchill had come to South Africa as a newspaper correspondent and made the mistake of being captured with a detachment of British soldiers and thrown into prison. Churchill was incensed at the failure of the Boers to discriminate between a journalist and a soldier and kept shouting that he was a reporter and therefore immune to capture. But Churchill was British and seemed to be with the British Army, so the Boers couldn't tell the difference. Churchill appealed to me in a few of his well-chosen words from the prison camp.*

I immediately set the machinery into motion for his release but before I could accomplish this legally, Churchill had escaped from prison. Long after, I met Churchill on some state occasion and recalled the incident.

"If you hadn't been so slow," Churchill told me, *"it would have cost me £9,000."*

£9,000?, I said.

"Yes, I wrote the story of my escape and sold it for that".'

*　　　*　　　*

He had a passion for pure English – whenever he saw the words 'concrete suggestion' he crossed out 'concrete' and substituted cement.

His derivation of a 'fanatic' was: *someone who can't change his mind and won't change the subject.*

He felt the maxim *'Nothing avails but perfection'* should be spelled *Paralysis.*

*　　　*　　　*

Churchill's genius for manipulating words quite often floored his political opponents in the Commons: This conversation took place in November 1947:

Churchill: *'Mr Herbert Morrison is a master of craftsmen.'*

Morrison: '*The right honourable Gentleman has promoted me.*'
Churchill: '*Craft is common both to skill and deceit.*'

*   *   *

'*I have been wondering, Mr Speaker, in all the circumstances, you would have permitted me to call this a lousy government, but I have concluded that it is not an adjective you would be willing to allow to be added to our Parliamentary vocabulary.*'

*   *   *

'*It (The Chinese Labour Contract) cannot in the opinion of His Majesty's Government be classified as slavery in the extreme acceptance of the word without some risk of terminological inexactitude.*'

*   *   *

The Minister of Food was about to establish 'communal feeding stations'. Churchill wrote in protest:

'*It is an odious expression suggestive of Communism and the workhouse. I suggest you call them "British restaurants". Everybody associates the word "restaurant" with a good meal, and they might as well have the name if they cannot get anything else.*'

*   *   *

'*I must now warn the House that I am going to make an unusual departure. I am going to make a Latin quotation. It is one which I hope will not offend the detachment of the old school tie. The quotation is Arma virumque cano, which, for the benefit of our *Winchester friends, I may translate as "Arms and the men I sing". That generally describes my theme.*'

At this point, Churchill was interrupted by Hugh Gaitskell, a Labour Party member:

* Gaitskell's school.

III

'*Should it not be man, the singular instead of the plural?*' he asked. Churchill replied:

'*Little did I expect that I should receive assistance on a classical matter from such a quarter.*'

– Commons, London. *March 1953*

* * *

'*I have always been very much struck by the advantage enjoyed by people who lived in an earlier period of the world than one's own.*

They had the opportunity of saying the right thing. Over and over again, it has happened to me to think of something which I thought was worth saying, only to find that it had been already exploited and very often spoiled before I had the opportunity of saying it.'

– Commons, London. *May 1927*

* * *

'*The advantages of the nineteenth century, the literary age, have been largely put away by this terrible twentieth century with all its confusion and exhaustion of mankind.*'

– University of London. *18th November 1948*

On Making
Speeches

On Making Speeches

Churchill, the legendary orator, once had a bad speech impediment. The specialist, consulted to cure the lisp, was told:

'Cure the impediment in my speech, please. I'm going into the army first. But as a minister later, I can't be haunted by the idea that I must avoid every word beginning with an s.'

* * *

'You can't make a speech on iced water.'

* * *

'Be on your guard! I am going to speak in French – a formidable undertaking and one which will put great demands upon your friendship for Great Britain.'

– To the French Assembly in Paris, after the Liberation

* * *

114

'*I had even noticed that the right honourable Gentleman always made a very good speech when he was in a very difficult position: the more there was to be said against the cause he was defending, the better the speech he made.*'

– *Commons, London. 24th February 1903*

*   *   *

Once asked what he thought of a certain statesman's speech on the League of Nations, Churchill said:

'*Well, I thought it was very good. It must have been good for it contained, so far as I know, all the platitudes known to the human race, with the possible exception of "Prepare to meet thy God" and "Please adjust your dress before leaving".*'

– *Commons, London. Between the two World Wars*

*   *   *

A very long speech from a new member of the House of Commons brought this comment:

'*I can understand the honourable member speaking for practice, which he sorely needs.*'

*   *   *

'*Most of all, I shall refrain from making any prediction upon the future. It is a month ago that I remarked upon the long silence of Herr Hitler, a remark which apparently provoked him to make a speech in which he told the German people that Moscow would fall in a few days.*

That shows, as everyone I am sure will agree, how much wiser he would have been to go on keeping his mouth shut.'

— *Commons, London. November 1941*

* * *

During his speech in the House of Commons, Sir William Joynson Hicks saw Winston Churchill shaking his head vigorously:

'I see my right honourable friend shaking his head. I wish to remind him that I am only expressing my own opinion.'

To which Churchill replied: *'And I wish to remind the speaker that I am only shaking my own head.'*

* * *

'Call that a maiden speech? It was a brazen hussy of a speech. Never did such a painted lady of a speech parade itself before a modest parliament!'

— *Commons, London. 1935*

* * *

Annoyed at the speech Churchill was making in the House of Commons, a member rose to protest but he was so incensed that the only sound he could emit was a strangled cry. Churchill's reaction was to say:

'My right honourable friend should not develop more indignation than he can contain.'

* * *

uffled against the cold and rain, Sir Winston leaves his Hyde Park Gate London home
: the House of Commons, 14th May 1963, after nearly a year's absence
m Parliament.

'My Darling Clementine' . . . Sir Winston and Lady Churchill on the occasion of Lady Churc

Birthday, 1st April 1963.

Sir Winston appears at the window of his London home on his 89th birthday;
30th November 1963.

'*I was taken to task the other day for saying that the Lord Privy Seal (Mr Eden) in his mission to the three capitals in Europe had failed. I have listened to his very agreeably delivered speech, so excellent in its phrasing and so well meant in its sentiments, and I am bound to say that the farthest I can go in altering my statement that his mission had failed is to say that up to the present, at any rate, it has not succeeded.*'

– Commons, London. 14th March 1934

*　　*　　*

In answer to an attack from Clement Attlee, Leader of the Opposition, Churchill said:

'*A great deal of his speech was made up of very effective points and quips which gave a great deal of satisfaction to those behind him. We all understand his position: "I am their leader, I must follow them".*'

– Commons, London. 1951

*　　*　　*

'*Lord Charles Beresford can best be described as one of those orators who, before they get up, do not know what they are going to say: when they are speaking, do not know what they are saying, and when they have sat down, do not know what they have said.*'

On Pastimes

On Pastimes

An artist of some considerable talent, one of Churchill's most loved pastimes was to paint landscapes. He took up this hobby during the First World War and said this of the event:

'And then it was that the Muse of Painting came to my rescue – out of charity and out of chivalry, because after all she had nothing to do with me – and said: "Are these toys any good for you? They amuse some people . . ."'

*   *   *

'I cannot pretend to feel impartial about colours. I rejoice with the brilliant ones and am genuinely sorry for the poor browns.'

*   *   *

'When I get to heaven I mean to spend a considerable portion of my first million years in painting, and so get to the bottom of the subject.

But then I shall require a still gayer palette than I get here below. I expect orange and vermillion will be the darkest, dullest colours upon it, and beyond them there will be a whole range of wonderful new colours which will delight the celestial eye.'

*　　*　　*

Bottlescapes *was the name Churchill gave to his paintings of bottles.*

*　　*　　*

Once asked why he always painted landscapes, Churchill replied:
   'Because a tree doesn't complain that I haven't done it justice.'

*　　*　　*

Another of Churchill's loves was for horses. He once advised:
   'Don't give your son money. As far as you can afford it, give him horses.'

*　　*　　*

   'I have always considered that the substitution of the internal combustion engine for the horse marked a very gloomy milestone in the progress of mankind.'

*　　*　　*

One of the horses from his racing stable at Chartwell Manor was *Colonist II*. Once when *Colonist II* was placed fourth in a race, Churchill was ready with a reason for his horse's poor showing. He said that he had had a serious talk with the horse just before the race:

'*I told him this is a very big race and if you win it, you will never have to run again. You will spend the rest of your life in agreeable female company.*' Then he added, '*Celonist 11 did not keep his mind on the race.*'

*   *   *

On the subject of alcohol he has had much to say, but about brandy in particular, he said:

'*I neither want it nor need it but I should think it pretty hazardous to interfere with the ineradicable habit of a lifetime.*'

*   *   *

'*I have always believed in the moderate and regular use of alcohol, especially under the conditions of winter war.*'

*   *   *

'*When I was a young subaltern in the South African War, the water was not fit to drink. To make it palatable, we had to add whisky. By diligent effort, I learned to like it.*'

        – Silver Spring, Maryland, USA, February 1947

*   *   *

'*All I can say is that I have taken more out of alcohol than alcohol has taken out of me!*'

On Religion

On Religion

'My various readings led me to ask myself questions about religion. Hitherto I had dutifully accepted everything I had been told. I had always had to go to church once a week. All this was very good. I accumulated in those years so fine a surplus in the Bank of Observance that I have been drawing confidently upon it ever since.'

* * *

'In the problems which the Almighty sets his humble servants things hardly ever happen the same way twice over, or, if they seem to do so, there is some variant which stultifies generalisations. The human mind, except when guided by extraordinary genius, cannot surmount the established conclusions amid which it has been reared.'

* * *

'*The Almighty in His infinite wisdom did not see fit to create Frenchmen in the image of Englishmen.*'

– December 1942

*   *   *

'*Will the Prime Minister assure the House,*' a Conservative member asked, '*that while we have quite properly attended to our physical needs of defence and of our other problems, we should not forget the spiritual resources which have inspired this country in the past and without which the noblest civilisation would decay.*'

'*I hardly think,*' the Prime Minister replied, '*that is my exclusive responsibility.*'

*   *   *

'*In the present age the State cannot control the Church in spiritual matters – it can only divorce it.*'

– Commons, London. 14th June 1928

*   *   *

During the Second World War the Archbishop of Canterbury had a makeshift bomb shelter in the crypt of Lambeth Palace. Concerned for the Archbishop's safety, Churchill made an inspection of the shelter and remarked:

'*This will never do. We must build a deeper and stronger shelter. But if, by chance, you should suffer a direct hit, I am afraid, my dear Archbishop, we will have to regard it as a Divine summons.*'

125

On Life

On Life

'*In one respect a cavalry charge is very like ordinary life. So long as you are all right, firmly in your saddle, your horse in hand, and well armed, lots of enemies will give you a wide berth. But as soon as you have lost a stirrup, have a rein cut, have dropped your weapon, are wounded or your horse is wounded, then is the moment when from all quarters enemies rush upon you.*'

* * *

'*Where does a family start? It starts with a young man falling in love with a girl – no superior alternative has yet been found.*'

* * *

'*Life is like going up a mountain. Each successive peak appears in turn the summit, and yet there is always another pinnacle beyond.*

– Commons, London. 31st July 1906

* * *

'*A young man cannot expect to get very far in life without getting some good smacks in the eye.*'

*   *   *

'*The human story does not always unfold like a mathematical calculation on the principle that two and two make four. Sometimes in life they make five or minus three; and sometimes the blackboard topples down in the middle of the sum and leaves the class in disorder and the pedagogue with a black eye.*'

*   *   *

'*There is all the difference in the world between a man who knocks you down and a man who leaves you alone.*'
— *Commons, London. 24th May 1944*

*   *   *

'*A bullet in the leg will make a brave man a coward. A blow on the head will make a wise man a fool. Indeed, I have read that a sufficiency of absinthe can make a good man a knave. The triumph of mind over matter does not seem to be quite completed yet.*'

*   *   *

There are two ways in which a gigantic debt may be spread over new decades and future generations.

There is the right and healthy way and there is the wrong and morbid way. The wrong way is to fail to make the utmost provision

for amortisation which prudence allows, to aggravate the burden of the debt by fresh borrowing, to live from hand to mouth, and from year to year, and to exclaim, with Louis XVI: 'After me, the deluge'.
 – Commons, London. April 1927

* * *

'It is a mistake to look too far ahead. Only one link in the chain of destiny can be handled at a time.'
 – Commons, London. 18th February 1945

* * *

'A hopeful disposition is not the sole qualification to be a prophet.'

* * *

'Spirits hold their own somewhat better under bleak conditions, but they must be expected in normal weather to resume their continuous descent.'
 – Commons, London. 24th April 1928

* * *

'Broadly speaking, human beings may be divided into three classes: those who are billed to death; those who are worried to death, and those who are bored to death.'

* * *

'*We have had to dispense with the indispensable.*'
— *Commons, London. 11th July 1922*

*   *   *

'*When you have to hold a coffee pot, it is better not to break the handle off until you are sure that you will get another equally convenient and serviceable, or, at any rate, until there is a dishcloth handy.*'
— *Commons, London. 22nd February 1944*

*   *   *

'*The oldest habit in the world for resisting change is to complain that unless the remedy to the disease can be universally applied it should not be applied at all. But you must begin somewhere.*'
— *Commons, London. 15th May 1911*

*   *   *

'*It is an important thing to diagnose the evil, but unless the malady be recognised it is idle to attempt to seek the remedy.*'
— *Commons, London. 21st June 1926*

*   *   *

'*You cannot cure cancer by a majority. What is needed is a remedy.*'
— *Commons, London. 11th June 1946*

*   *   *

'*Evils can be created much quicker than they can be cured.*'
— *Liverpool. 2nd October 1951*

*   *   *

'*When I survey in the light of these reflections the scene of my past life as a whole, I have no doubt that I do not wish to live it over again. Happy, vivid and full of interest as it has been. I do not seek to tread again the toilsome and dangerous path. Not even an opportunity of making a different set of mistakes and experiencing a different set of adventures and successes would lure me. How can I tell that the good fortune which has up to the present attended me with fair constancy would not be lacking at some critical moment in another chain of causation?*'

On Danger, Defeat and Death

On Danger, Defeat and Death

'Nothing in life is so exhilarating as to be shot at without result.'

*   *   *

'The air is an extremely dangerous mistress. Once under the spell, most lovers are faithful to the end, which is not always old age.'

*   *   *

'It is very much better, sometimes, to have a panic feeling beforehand, and then be quite calm when things happen, than to be extremely calm beforehand and go into panic when things happen.'
– Commons, London. May 1935

*   *   *

'The only answer to defeat is victory.'
– Commons, London. 10th June 1941

*   *   *

'*The problems of victory are more agreeable than those of defeat, but they are no less difficult.*'

*　　*　　*

Whilst campaigning for the 1922 election, Churchill was admitted to hospital for an appendectomy. He lost the election and afterwards described his position as:

'*Without an office, without a seat, without a party and without an appendix.*'

*　　*　　*

Defeated again in 1945, his wife Clementine tried to cheer him up by saying:

'*It may well be a blessing in disguise.*'

He answered, wryly:

'*At the moment, it seems quite effectively disguised.*'

*　　*　　*

Whilst defending the death sentence on the grounds that hanging, under English Law, if properly conducted was an absolutely painless death, Churchill was interrupted by an MP who asked him to 'try it'.

'*Well, it may come to that*', Churchill replied.

– *Commons, London. 1948*

*　　*　　*

'*Although always prepared for martyrdom, I preferred that it should be postponed.*'

*　　*　　*

When he was seventy-five he was asked if he had any fear of death:

'*I am ready to meet my Maker,*' he replied quietly, '*whether my Maker is prepared for the great ordeal of meeting me is another matter.*'

Acknowledgements

The compiler wishes to acknowledge his indebtedness to the authors and publishers of the following works:

As It Happened, (Lord Attlee: Heinemann); *F E*, (The Earl of Birkenhead: Eyre and Spottiswoode); *The War and Colonel Warden*, (Gerald Pawle: Harrap); *The Wit of Sir Winston*, (Ed. Adam Sykes and Iain Sproat: Leslie Frewin); *The Wit of Winston Churchill*, (Ed. Bill Adler: Citadel Press, New York); *My Years with Churchill*, (Norman McGowan: Souvenir Press); *My Yesterday, Your Tomorrow*, (Lord Boothby: Hutchinson); *Thoughts and Adventures*, (W S Churchill: Thornton Butterworth) *The Prof in Two Worlds*, (The Earl of Birkenhead: Collins); *The Finest Hours*, (Jack Le Vien: Corgi); *The Wit of Winston*

Churchill, (Ed. Geoffrey Williams and Charles Roetter: Max Parrish); *Churchill the Great,* (Victor Sim: *Daily Mirror* Newspapers); *Randolph Churchill Remembers,* (London *Sunday Times*); *Old Men Forget,* (Duff Cooper: Heinemann); *Headlines All My Life,* (Arthur Christiansen: Heinemann); *Mr Churchill in 1940,* (Isaiah Berlin: John Murray); *My Darling Clementine,* (Jack Fishman: W H Allen); *Five Lives,* (The Earl of Longford: Hutchinson); *New Statesmanship,* (Ed. Edward Hyams: Longmans); *War Speeches:* Three Volumes, (Ed. Charles Eade: Cassell and Co); *Stemming The Tide:* Speeches, (Ed. Randolph S Churchill: Cassell and Co); *Victory:* War Speeches, (Ed. Charles Eade: Cassell and Co); *Into Battle:* Speeches, (Ed. Randolph S Churchill: Cassell and Co); *Painting as a Pastime,* (Winston S Churchill: Ernest Benn); *The Second World War:* Six Volumes, (Winston S Churchill: Cassell and Co) and *Hansard.*

Thanks are also due to the editors of the London *Daily Telegraph, Sunday Telegraph, The Times, Daily Express, Sunday Express, Sunday Times,* and the following photographic sources:

Keystone Press Agency Limited
The War Office
Society and General Press Agency
PA Reuters Photos.
United Press International (UK) Limited